y

EXPRESSIONISM

A clear insight into Artists and their Art

Pam Cutler

Barrington Stoke

First published 2004 in Great Britain by
Barrington Stoke Ltd, Sandeman House, Trunk's Close,
55 High Street, Edinburgh, EH1 1SR

www.barringtonstoke.co.uk

Front cover image: Friedrichstrasse, 1914 by Ernst Ludwig
Kirchner Tate, London, UK

ISBN 1-84299-179-5

Edited by Julia Rowlandson
Cover design by Helen Ferguson
Picture research by Kate MacPhee

Designed and typeset by GreenGate Publishing Services,
Tonbridge
Printed in Great Britain by The Bath Press

Barrington Stoke acknowledges support from the Scottish
Arts Council towards the publication of this title.

Scottish
Arts Council
LOTTERY FUNDED

Contents

Introduction

At the beginning of the 20th century, artists did not want to limit themselves to making pictures that looked like the real world. They thought that the new technology of photography could do this well, leaving artists free to use their imaginations to produce new forms of art.

These artists wanted to express their inner thoughts and feelings. They tried out bold *compositions* and vivid colours. Their new ways of looking at the world often upset art critics and the public.

The most important Expressionist paintings were created between 1905 and 1914 but by 1920 the influence of the Expressionist movement had faded. All the Expressionist artists were affected by World War I and, sadly, some were killed. All the same, their work inspired artists throughout the 20th century and contributed to the development of modern art.

In order to understand more about Expressionism, we need to discover the answers to the following five questions:

- Where did Expressionism come from?
- What was Expressionism?
- Who were the Expressionists?
- What and who influenced Expressionist artists to work in the way they did?
- What did the Expressionists like to paint and what methods did they use?

PART ONE

Where did Expressionism come from?

Developments in France

The state of the arts was very different from other European countries. In France, new developments in art were always seen at the major exhibitions in Paris. Artists met each other in the cafés of Paris and shared ideas on art. The critics wrote about the latest developments and new ways of painting developed out of previous styles. The French art world was very lively and artists competed with each other to become the next leader of an *avant-garde* movement.

In 1905, when **Henri Matisse** and his friends showed their latest paintings at the *Salon d'Automne*, Matisse became the leader of a new avant-garde movement called *Fauvism*. The *Fauves* shocked the public with their rich use of colour and bold shapes. Their style was a dramatic development of the work of the Post-Impressionist artists **Vincent Van Gogh**, **Georges Seurat**, **Paul Gauguin** and **Paul Cézanne**.

avant-garde – a military term which was given to the art movement which was the most recent, shocking and innovative.

Fauvism / Fauves – comes from a French word meaning 'wild beasts'. In 1905, this name was given to a group of artists led by Henri Matisse who painted using a bold and shocking style with very bright colours.

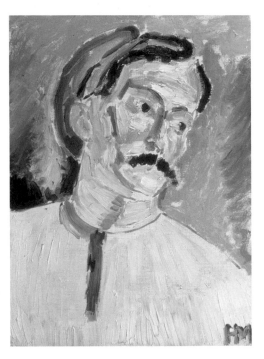

Portrait of André Derain (1905) by Henri Matisse
Tate, London, UK. © 2004 Succession H. Matisse/DACS 2004

Jugendstil – the art nouveau movement in Germany was called Jugendstil after a magazine called *Jugend* or *Youth* which was first published in 1896.

Art Nouveau – the term means 'new art' and this movement spread across Europe and America in the 1890s. It was mainly a style of architecture and interior decoration and was based on flat patterns and organic forms.

Developments in Germany

In **Germany**, the Kaiser, or Emperor of Germany, ruled over the whole country and he made sure that artists painted subjects from history and pictures which praised his reign. By the 1890s, artists were getting fed up with these tight controls on art and began to break away from the established academies of art and set up their own groups and schools.

These break-away groups were called *Secessions* (the word 'secede' means to break away or stop being a member of something). Each major German city, such as Munich, Dresden and Berlin, developed their own styles and ways of doing things.

Munich became the centre of a new Arts and Crafts movement which developed a way of designing which was called *Jugendstil*. This was led by the artist **Franz Von Stuck** and was the German version of the *Art Nouveau* movement. It encouraged artists to make simplified designs from pure natural forms. Kandinsky (see page 38) studied under Franz von Stuck at the Munich Academy of Art and founded a group called the **Phalanx** in 1901. This group organised exhibitions of French Impressionist and Post-Impressionist work.

In Berlin, a painter called **Max Liebermann** led a group of artists who wanted to rebel. He encouraged young German artists to take part in the Paris International Exhibition of 1889. He also set up international exhibitions in Berlin. In 1902, there was an exhibition which showed 28 pictures by the Norwegian artist **Edvard Munch**, and, in 1903 an exhibition of the Post-Impressionist artists, **Van Gogh**, **Gauguin** and **Cézanne**.

The young artists who formed the Expressionist groups, **Die Brücke** and **Der Blaue Reiter**, were drawn to these exciting centres where they could meet other artists who were keen on new artistic ideas.

Developments in Austria

In **Austria**, as in Germany, young artists wanted to try out new methods and subjects in their paintings. They were fed up with the *traditional* methods of the old academies and started setting up their own schools.

One of the most well-known of these groups of artists was called the Vienna *Secession* which was set up in 1897. It was made up of artists, sculptors, architects and designers who worked together on projects. One of the leading artists was **Gustav Klimt** (1862–1918). Klimt encouraged two younger artists called **Egon Schiele** (1890–1918) and **Oskar Kokoschka** (1886–1980) who both painted people in an Expressionist way using *distortion* and *exaggerated* gestures.

tradition, traditional – ways of doing things which are often handed down from one generation to another.

distort, distortion – to twist or stretch something into a different shape to deform it.

exaggerated – overstated and emphasised.

What was Expressionism?

'Expressionism' is not the name of a particular art movement. It is a term which describes the work of several groups of artists who developed new ways of making pictures in the early 20th century. They wanted their paintings to be full of energy and expression and believed that art could change people's lives.

People do not agree about when the term 'Expressionism' was first used. Some people think that the critic, Louis Vauxcelles, was the first to use it to describe the paintings of **Henri Matisse** (see page 20) and his friends. In 1905, they showed their new work at the *Salon d'Automne*, and he said their pictures were 'Expressionist' and looked like the work of 'wild beasts' or *Fauves*.

catalogue – a book which lists artworks displayed in an exhibition and also has essays in it describing and explaining the work.

Cubism / Cubists – a style of painting developed in 1908 by Georges Braque and Pablo Picasso. They made paintings which showed things from different angles at the same time and broke up their pictures into geometric shapes like cubes and triangles.

Futurism / Futurists – the Futurists were a group of Italian artists, such as Giacomo Balla and Umberto Boccioni, who were working around 1909. They loved big cities, speed and machinery and tried to show dynamic movement in their paintings.

Blaue Reiter – the term means Blue Rider. Kandinsky and Marc organised two Blaue Reiter exhibitions in 1911 and 1912. They also published the Blaue Reiter almanac in May, 1912.

The word 'Expressionism' was also in the *catalogue* of the famous Sonderbund Exhibition held in Cologne in 1912. This was an international exhibition which showed new work from across Europe including the French *Cubists* and Italian *Futurists*. The **Die Brücke** artists, **Ernst Kirchner** and **Erich Heckel**, also showed paintings in this exhibition and were asked to decorate the chapel attached to the exhibition building.

The catalogue said that the aim of the Sonderbund Exhibition was to provide a survey of the movement known as 'Expressionism'. It said that the artists on display shared certain aims. These were 'to simplify and intensify the forms of expression, to achieve new rhythm and colourfulness, to create in decorative or monumental forms'.

The leader of the *Blaue Reiter* group, **Wassily Kandinsky**, also talked about Expressionism in his essay *On the Spiritual in Art* (1911). He said they wanted to show nature as a form of 'inner impression which has recently been called Expression'.

Today, people still argue about 'Expressionism'. Some people think that only the artists in Germany, like the *Blaue Reiter* and *Die Brücke* artists, should be called 'Expressionists'. Others think it is a more general term to describe the work of artists who used colour and shape in a new and expressive way, and created bold pictures which shocked the world during the years 1905 to the beginning of World War I in 1914.

Who were the Expressionists?

The Expressionist movement included artists from across Europe. The main artists were as follows:

- In France, the *Fauves* included **Henri Matisse**, **André Derain**, **Maurice De Vlaminck** and **Albert Marquet**.

- In Germany, there were two main groups:

  1. The *Die Brücke* artists were based in Dresden and then Berlin. They included **Ernst Ludwig Kirchner**, **Karl Shmidt-Rottluff**, **Erich Heckel**, **Max Pechstein** and **Otto Mueller**. **Emil Nolde** was also in the group for a short time.

  2. The *Blaue Reiter* group was based in Munich and included **Wassily Kandinsky**, **Franz Marc**, **Alexei Von Jawlensky**, **Gabriele Munter** and **Marianne Von Werefkin**. **August Macke** was a close friend of Marc's and contributed to the ideas of the group.

  There was also another group of artists in Germany which included **Max Beckmann**, **George Grosz** and **Otto Dix**. They reacted against Expressionism and set up the *New Objectivity* movement in the 1920s.

- In Austria, two artists were important in the Expressionist movement in Vienna. They were **Oskar Kokoschka** and **Egon Schiele**.

New Objectivity – an art movement in Germany which reacted against Expressionism. The main painters were George Grosz, Otto Dix and Max Beckmann. They wanted art to be more realistic and political.

What and who influenced the Expressionists to work in the way they did?

At the beginning of the 20th century, artists were searching for new and more meaningful ways to express themselves. Some were sure they were on the brink of a new spiritual age and believed that art could take a leading role in expressing the exciting ideas of a new century.

In their search for a more direct and purer form of expression they studied folk art and explored art from Africa and the South Pacific. Kandinsky's *Blaue Reiter* almanac showed art work from all over the world including Chinese paintings, sculpture from Mexico, Cameroon and the Easter Islands, Japanese pen and ink drawings, Russian folk prints and Egyptian shadow-play figures.

International exhibitions were organised in all the major cities of Europe and artists had better chances to share their ideas with artists from other countries.

The influence of the Post-Impressionists

One of the biggest influences on the artistic styles of Expressionist artists was the work of the four main Post-Impressionist artists, **Georges Seurat**, **Paul Gauguin**, **Paul Cézanne** and **Vincent Van Gogh**.

They admired the *vibrant* effect that Seurat achieved in paintings like **Seascape at Port-en-Bessin** (1888) when he put dashes of pure colour side by side. They were influenced by Gauguin's expressive and *symbolic* use of colour (**Words of the Devil**, 1892) and Van Gogh's intensely personal approach to colour and brushwork (**The Church at Auvers**, 1890). Paintings like Cézanne's **Landscape with Rocks and Trees** (1895) inspired painters to think of colour and shape as being expressive in themselves.

vibrant – vivid, thrilling.

symbolic / symbolist – a sign or object which stands in for, and refers to, a hidden or deeper meaning. The Symbolist movement involved writers as well as artists. Symbolists were against realism in Art and wanted to create pictures which were more imaginative and dream-like.

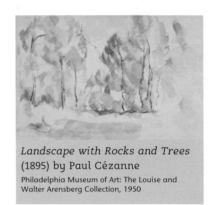

Landscape with Rocks and Trees (1895) by Paul Cézanne
Philadelphia Museum of Art: The Louise and Walter Arensberg Collection, 1950

Seascape at Port-en-Bessin (1888) by Georges Seurat
Musée d'Orsay, Paris

The Church at Auvers (1890) by
Vincent Van Gogh
Musée d'Orsay, Paris, France

Words of the Devil (1892) by
Paul Gauguin
Gift of the W. Averell Harriman Foundation in
memory of Marie N. Harriman

The Scream (1893) by Edvard Munch
Nasjonalgalleriet, Oslo, Norway, © Munch
Museum/Munch - Ellingsen Group, BONO, Oslo,
DACS, London 2004

psychology – a study of
human behaviour and states of
mind.

rhythm, rhythmic – a flow
of words, music, or colours and
shapes in which there are
repeated weak and strong
elements.

composition – arrangement of
the parts of a picture.

dynamic / dynamism – full
of movement, spirited and
powerful.

The influence of Edvard Munch

The Norwegian artist, **Edvard Munch**, came to Paris in
1889 and was inspired by the work of **Toulouse-Lautrec**,
Van Gogh and **Gauguin**. His work had a strong
emotional content and *psychological* tension. He created
terrifying images of fear in paintings like **The Scream**
(1893). His startling colour contrasts and *rhythmic* lines
seem to spread a feeling of nightmarish panic
throughout the painting.

Munch had several exhibitions of his work in Germany
in the early years of the 20th century and had a strong
influence on **Emil Nolde** (see page 16) and the Die Brücke
artists.

The influence of other art forms

The impact of Expressionism was felt in all the arts
including theatre, literature and music. Kirchner admired
Alfred Doblin's Expressionist novel about city life called
Berlin Alexanderplatz. Kandinsky was inspired by the
music of modern composers like **Schonberg** and **Stravinsky**
and felt his own paintings could be experienced like music
as *dynamic, rhythmic compositions*. He also wrote works
for the stage such as *Violet Curtain*, 1914.

13

What did the Expressionists like to paint and what methods did they use?

Expressionist artists believed that painting their own impressions and feelings was far more important than recording what things looked like but their methods of doing this varied a lot:

In France

Fauvism

Henri Matisse

Matisse contrasted flat areas of pure colour to create decorative scenes and landscapes. His bold brushstrokes and bright unnatural colours gave the effect of *vibrant* light in **Open Window, Collioure,** 1905 (see page 26).

vibrant – vivid, thrilling.

Maurice de Vlaminck

Vlaminck admired Van Gogh's powerful expressive use of colour. He used energetic and swirling brushstrokes as well as vivid colour contrasts to create **The Seine at Pecq,** 1905.

André Derain

Mountains at Collioure, 1905, shows the influence of Van Gogh in the long strokes of pure colour which he uses to describe the trees and grass. He also painted *vibrant* landscapes like **Boats in the Port of Collioure,** 1905, using short, swift dashes of colours which were not true to nature.

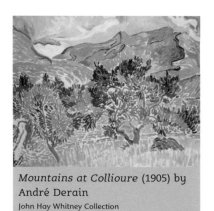

Mountains at Collioure (1905) by André Derain
John Hay Whitney Collection

rhythm, rhythmic – a flow of words, music, or colours and shapes in which there are repeated weak and strong elements.

distort, distortion – to twist or stretch something into a different shape to deform it.

perspective – a way of constructing a picture from a particular viewpoint as though you were looking through a window into it.

complementary colours – colours opposite each other in the colour wheel which create a vibrant effect when placed near to one another. These complementary colours included red/green, yellow/purple and blue/orange.

Railway in Berlin (1911) by Erich Heckel
Museum Abteiberg Mönchengladbach, Germany, © DACS 2004

In Germany

1 Die Brücke (The Bridge)

The Die Brücke group wanted 'freedom for their hands and lives'. They thought they should follow their instincts rather than think everything out and wanted their pictures to be energetic and direct. Their drawings and woodcut prints were often basic, aggressive and emotional. They shared the same studio and lived and worked together. They often went on painting trips together and their favourite subject was man in a natural environment far away from factories and industry. The methods of four of the *Die Brücke* painters are as follows:

Ernst Ludwig Kirchner

Kirchner made the shapes of things simpler and put dark outlines around them. His paintings of nudes like **Stepping Gingerly into the Sea**, 1912 have strong *rhythmic* shapes and unnatural colours. In his paintings of city life, like **Potsdamer Platz, Berlin**, 1914 (see page 36), his people stand in cramped, *distorted* spaces. His shapes are pointed and aggressive and he slashes the canvas with energetic brushstrokes.

Erich Heckel

Heckel painted his immediate impressions as directly as possible with swift brush strokes. He thinned his paint with petrol and other thinners so that he could spread it more quickly. In the landscape **Windmill near Dangast**, 1909, he used strong contrasts of *complementary colours*, and painted the landscape with bold blocks of colour rather than using *perspective* drawing. His paintings of nudes and menacing pictures of the city (**Railway in Berlin**, 1911) were bold and effective because of their flat, simple shapes and strong colour contrasts.

Karl Schmidt-Rottluff

Schmidt-Rottluff painted striking portraits with bold patches of *unnaturalistic* colours as in **Portrait of Rosa Schapire**, 1911. He was influenced by *Cubism* and African sculptures as in **Double Portrait S and L**, 1925, where the faces have dark outlines and look like carved masks.

Emil Nolde

Nolde joined Die Brücke for a short time although his work was very different. He was a deeply religious man and his painting of the **Crucifixion**, 1912, is stark and emotional. He *distorted* and *exaggerated* the bodies of his figures and painted their faces like masks. He was influenced by the intense colours of Van Gogh and the emotional content of Edvard Munch's **The Scream**, 1893 (see page 13).

2 *Der Blaue Reiter*

The Blaue Reiter artists wanted their paintings to express the spiritual side of life and thought that their art could bring together ideas from philosophy, religion and music. Their methods were as follows:

Wassily Kandinsky

Kandinsky's first paintings were based on the folk art of Russia and Germany and then he worked towards totally *abstract* paintings like **Black Strokes I**, 1913 (see page 17). These were *dynamic compositions* of floating areas of bright colour and expressive lines and shapes. He wanted his *rhythmic* use of colour and form to create a visual experience which was like music.

---

unnaturalistic – unrealistic method that does not attempt to show nature as it is.

exaggerated – overstated and emphasised.

abstract / abstraction – abstract art calls attention to shape, colour and form rather than making an object or landscape look recognisable.

dynamic / dynamism – full of movement, spirited and powerful.

rhythm, rhythmic – a flow of words, music, or colours and shapes in which there are repeated weak and strong elements.

Crucifixion (1912) by Emil Nolde
© Nolde-Stiftung Seebull

Black Strokes 1 (1913) by Wassily Kandinsky
Soloman R. Guggenheim Museum, New York. Gift, Solomon R. Guggenheim

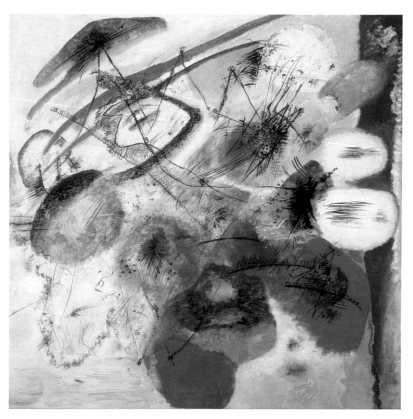

Cubism / Cubists – a style of painting developed in 1908 by Georges Braque and Pablo Picasso. They made paintings which showed things from different angles at the same time and broke up their pictures into geometric shapes like cubes and triangles.

composition – arrangement of the parts of a picture.

Tiger (1912) by Franz Marc
Stadtische Galerie im Lenbachhaus, Munich, Germany

Franz Marc
Marc painted imaginative and colourful compositions showing animals at one with nature. He was influenced by *Cubism* and broke down the forms of animals and their surroundings into geometric shapes. In **Tiger**, 1912, he created a vivid picture of a pure world untouched by man.

Alexei von Jawlensky
In landscapes like **Solitude**, 1912, Jawlensky, painted striking *compositions* of simplified forms, vivid colours and decorative lines.

3 Art and the City

Max Beckmann, George Grosz and **Otto Dix**, although
they headed the *New Objectivity* movement, are
sometimes thought of as Expressionist artists. After their
experiences in World War I, they produced nightmarish
pictures showing the aggression and violence of
mankind. In **The Dream**, 1921, Max Beckmann showed
ugly figures in a cramped, *distorted* space.

In Austria

Vienna Secession

Gustav Klimt

Klimt was one of the founding members of the Vienna
Secession. His most famous painting, **The Kiss**
(1907–1908), is disturbing and beautiful at the same
time. A man and woman are joined together in a deep
embrace. Their poses are awkward and angular and
they are hidden beneath robes of rich golden mosaic.

Egon Schiele

Egon Schiele was a young student of Klimt. He made
disturbing drawings of the human body which were
tense and *distorted* like his **Self-Portrait with Black
Earthenware Vessel**, 1911.

Oskar Kokoschka

Kokoschka painted striking and expressive portraits. His
people have long nervous hands and motionless faces
(**Portrait of Hans Tietze and Erica Tietze-Conrat**, 1909).

The Kiss (1907–1908) by
Gustav Klimt
Osterreichische Galerie Belvedere, Vienna, Austria

Biographies of Artists and their Paintings Explored

PART
TWO

Self-portrait (1918) by
Henri Matisse
Musee Matisse, Le Cateau-Cambresis, France,
© Succession H. Matisse / DACS 2004

Born: 31st December 1869
Died: 3rd November 1954
Place of Birth: Le Chateau-Cambresis in north-eastern France
Family details: Matisse's parents owned a general store selling household goods and grain. Matisse was the eldest of three children.
Paintings analysed:
Open Window, Collioure, 1905

HENRI MATISSE

Childhood and youth

porcelain – delicate kind of clay from which statues or fine china can be made.

symbolic / symbolist – a sign or object which stands in for, and refers to, a hidden or deeper meaning. The Symbolist movement involved writers as well as artists. Symbolists were against realism in Art and wanted to create pictures which were more imaginative and dream-like.

When Henri Matisse was a boy, his parents thought that he would run their large general store when he grew up. He went to boarding school at Saint Quentin for five years and, when he was seventeen, he studied Law in Paris. After two years, he passed his exams and started working as a lawyer's assistant.

In 1889, Matisse fell ill with appendicitis and had to spend almost a year in bed. His mother who loved painting *porcelain* bought her son a box of paints to pass the time. Matisse had already shown an interest in art and had gone to drawing classes while he was working in the lawyer's office, but now he realised he loved to paint more than anything else. When he was well again he did not go back to his Law career but became a student of art at the Academie Julian in Paris. His father thought he was making a big mistake but his mother supported him.

Early career in art

By 1895, Matisse was a student of the famous *Symbolist* painter, Gustave Moreau, at the Ecole des Beaux-Arts. He studied Old Masters in the Museums of Paris and started exhibiting and selling some of his paintings. He soon found the work of the Impressionist painters, and in 1897, he exhibited **Dinner Table**, 1897, which showed his new focus on light effects and colour.

In 1898, he married Amelie Parayre and they had three children. Although Matisse was beginning to sell his paintings, the family was still very poor and were often ill. Amelie worked as a hatmaker and Matisse took a job as a scene painter in the theatre.

Dinner Table (1897) by Henri Matisse
Private Collection, © Succession H. Matisse / DACS 2004

In 1900, he was asked to decorate the Grand Palais for the Great Exhibition with his painter friend, **Albert Marquet**. He also exhibited work at the *Salon des Indépendants* and started meeting painters like **Paul Signac**, **Maurice de Vlaminck** and **André Derain**. They were all influenced by the *Divisionist* colour work of **Georges Seurat**. Matisse already admired the work of other *Post-Impressionist* artists and owned one of **Van Gogh**'s drawings as well as paintings by **Gauguin** and **Cézanne**.

By 1903, Matisse's work was becoming more well-known. He showed paintings at the first *Salon d'Automne* Exhibition and had a one-man show at the *avant-garde* Ambroise Vollard Gallery. In 1904 he painted **Luxe, Calme et Volupté**, in the *Divisionist* style with dashes of pure, bright colour.

avant-garde – a military term which was given to the art movement which was the most recent, shocking and innovative.

perspective – a way of constructing a picture from a particular viewpoint as though you were looking through a window into it.

Fauvism and the development of Matisse's career

In the summer of 1905 Matisse made a breakthrough in his style of painting. He was staying with his family and artist friends, **Maurice de Vlaminck** and **André Derain**, in the small fishing village of Collioure in the south of France. They experimented with bold, new ways of using colour, shapes and pattern. They were not interested in *perspective* or using colours to show the natural appearance of things. Instead they wanted to show how colours and shapes could be expressive by themselves. In Matisse's **Portrait of André Derain**, 1905 (see page 6) he uses striking contrasts of *complementary colours* to create a powerful image of his friend.

Luxe, Calme et Volupté (1904) by Henri Matisse

Musee d'Orsay, Paris, France, © Succession H. Matisse / DACS 2004

Not many people understood or liked their paintings when they showed them at the *Salon d'Automne* in 1905. The critic, Louis Vauxcelles, thought they looked like the work of *fauves* or wild beasts because the drawings were so sketchy and the colours so bright and vivid. The artists were not put off and they thought it was good that their work had caused such a sensation.

patrons – people who support artists by promoting and buying their work.

composition – arrangement of the parts of a picture.

They decided to go on calling themselves *Fauves* and Matisse was seen as the leader of the new art movement called *Fauvism*.

The ideas and techniques of *Fauvism* were taken up by many modern artists of the 20th century and had a big influence on many of the Expressionist painters in Germany including **Kirchner** and **Kandinsky**.

New directions in Matisse's work

Rich *patrons* like the Gertrude Stein family in America and the Russian businessman, Sergei Schukin, started buying Matisse's work. Leo Stein bought Matisse's famous painting, **La Joie de Vivre** (1905–1906), and Schukin asked him to paint two large murals called **Dance** and **Music** (1909–1910) for his house in Moscow.

During the years 1906 to 1910, Matisse travelled a lot visiting North Africa and many European countries. He admired the work from other cultures including African and South Pacific sculpture as well as Arabic art and Oriental carpets. He began making his own sculpture (**Two Women**, 1907) and became much more interested in decorative pattern in his paintings (**Harmony in Red**, 1908).

In 1912 he made two long trips to Morocco in North Africa and his paintings from this period have more simple *compositions* and a new sense of light and calm (**Entrance to the Kasbah**, 1912).

Harmony in Red (1908) by Henri Matisse
Hermitage Museum Saint Petersburg, Russia,
© Succession H. Matisse / DACS 2004

Dance (1909–1910) by Henri Matisse
Hermitage, St. Petersburg, Russia, © Succession H. Matisse / DACS 2004

Music (1909–1910) by Henri Matisse
Hermitage, St. Petersburg, Russia, © Succession H. Matisse / DACS 2004

In 1914, when World War I started, Matisse was 45 years old and was not asked to join the French Army. An exhibition of his paintings in Berlin was taken by the German authorities and not returned. Throughout the war, Matisse went on working and had exhibitions in Paris and New York. In 1918, he painted his **Self-portrait** showing himself as a neatly-dressed, serious man who spent long hours painting at his easel. (See page 20.)

Matisse's career after World War I

In 1920, Matisse designed the set and costumes for a ballet called 'The Nightingale' by the famous Russian composer, Stravinsky. During the 1920s, Matisse painted a series of *Odalisques* which show women in relaxed poses surrounded by beautiful Oriental carpets and tapestries (**Odalisque in Red Trousers**, 1924–1925). By now he was a very well-known and successful painter and, in 1930, an American art collector called Alfred Barnes asked him to paint a wall-painting of dancers for the Barnes Foundation at Merion in America.

Odalisques – the name given to female slaves from Turkish harems. In Matisse's work the term refers to a series of paintings of reclining women in exotic surroundings.

On the whole, the 1930s were not good years for Matisse. He was ill and had split up from his wife, Amelie. He continued to work hard making simple and striking compositions. In 1940, one year after the start of World War II, he had a major operation for cancer. He was 71 years old.

Odalisque in Red Trousers (1924–1925) by Henri Matisse
Musee National d'Art Moderne - Centre Pompidou, Paris, France, © Succession H. Matisse / DACS 2004

The final years of Matisse's life

In 1945, when World War II was over, Matisse came back to Paris and had two big exhibitions at the *Salon D'Automne* and the Victoria and Albert Museum in London. He was still very weak from his illness so he started a new way of working which he called 'drawing with scissors'. Using this method, Matisse made some wonderful designs like **The Circus**, 1947 and published them in a book called *Jazz* in 1947. In 1948, he used the same method to create stunning designs in blue, green and yellow for a stained glass widow at the Chapel of the Rosary in Venice.

In 1950, when he was 81 years old, he was awarded the Grand Prix at the Venice Biennale which is one of the largest festivals of modern art. He still carried on working and, in 1953, produced the painted paper cut-out called **The Snail**, which was to become one of the most famous works of 20th century art.

The next year, on 3rd November 1954, Henri Matisse died of a heart attack just before his 85th birthday. In the years before his death, Matisse helped to set up a museum of his work in the town where he was born at Le Chateau-Cambresis in north-east France. This museum is now a wonderful record of his outstanding career and contribution to modern art.

The Snail (1953) by Henri Matisse
Tate, London, UK, © Succession H. Matisse / DACS 2004

Open Window, Collioure, 1905, by Henri Matisse

Background

In 1905, Matisse and his family spent the summer in Collioure, a fishing village in south-west France. Two younger artists, André Derain and Maurice Vlaminck, met up with him there and they developed their new ideas on painting together. They all admired the *Post-Impressionist* artists and Matisse had just helped to put up a large exhibition of Van Gogh's paintings which made him want to paint more freely and use more expressive colours.

Open Window, Collioure, 1905, is one of the first Fauve works to be painted. (See page 22.)

Matisse explained what he was trying to do: 'What I am after, above all is expression. Expression does not consist of the passion mirrored upon a human face. The whole arrangement of my picture is expressive. The placement of figures or objects, the empty spaces around them, the proportions, everything plays a part'. This new way of painting, '*Fauvism*', influenced many Expressionist artists in Germany including Kandinsky and Kirchner.

Ideas

- Paint a landscape using colours as close to nature as you can. Then paint it again changing the colours to different combinations of vivid *complementary colours* such as red/green, yellow/purple and blue/orange.

- Matisse loved painting rooms with windows in them opening onto a garden or landscape. Paint two versions of your own view through a window. In the first one, construct your picture using *one-point perspective* to create a sense of distance. In the second, record the landscape using shape and colour alone.

  Try to make the colours inside your room balance out the ones in your landscape and use *complementary colours* to create a vivid effect.

- In later paintings like **Odalisque in Red Trousers**, 1924–1925, Matisse developed his love of pattern. Collect together lots of patterned and decorative material. Arrange them on a sofa or chair and ask one of your friends to sit or lie down amongst them. When painting your scene take care to show how folds in the material change the pattern.

Content

Through an open window you can see the harbour at Collioure. Brightly coloured sailing boats bob around in the pink sea. On the balcony, there are pots full of red geranium flowers. Matisse has painted everything with bright contrasting colours which create a *vibrant* effect of light and life.

Throughout his life, Matisse often painted rooms with windows looking out onto a garden or landscape. **Interior at Collioure (The Rest)**, painted around the same time in 1905–1906, shows a room in which his wife, Amelie, lies resting on a bed. Through the window in this picture you can see their daughter standing on the balcony watching what is going on in the harbour below.

In a later work, **Harmony in Red,** 1908–1909 (see page 23), Matisse shows a woman arranging fruit on a table. Through the window in this picture you can see a garden with trees in flower. Matisse's style has become much more decorative and there is not much sense of depth. The pattern of the tablecloth continues up the walls and the garden in the window looks like a flat pattern too.

Form

Matisse's picture is made up of four different frames or windows. The walls on each side frame the glass windows. These frame the balcony which frames the harbour view. Matisse shows us a view onto the world outside the window and at the same time creates a *composition* of flat, patterned surfaces.

The colours he used in his picture do not describe the real appearance of things. He chose colours which were the same tone as the real thing but not the same *hue* (tint). He said, 'When I put a green, it is not grass. When I put a blue, it is not the sky'. In **Open Window**, Matisse painted the boats bobbing around on pink waves under a sky streaked with mauve and turquoise. The blue-green and vivid red colours inside the room are surprising too.

Although the critics thought his paintings were wild, Matisse really wanted to create a *harmonious* balance of colours which would be as pleasing as music. Areas of red and green *complementary colours* balance each other out. The potted plants and vine growing around the balcony are painted in *rhythmic* dashes of brilliant colour.

Process

Matisse constructed his painting with areas of pure, bright colour which are not blended into each other.

His varied brushstrokes create different surface areas. He uses short, squiggly marks around the balcony; flat, sweeping brushstrokes on the walls; and long thin streaks of paint for the sea and sky.

Matisse's use of *complementary colours* creates a strong sense of light. The boats are deep blue with orange masts. The pinks and reds of the walls and window panes contrast with areas of blue-green to make a *vibrant* effect.

Mood

Matisse said that he wanted to create a 'living harmony of colours', and in this *vibrant* painting, he has succeeded. It has a warm atmosphere which is full of the joy of life.

It is at the edge of *abstraction*. In one way it creates the illusion of space as you look through the window at the harbour below and, in another way, it is an attractive *composition* of coloured shapes and patterns.

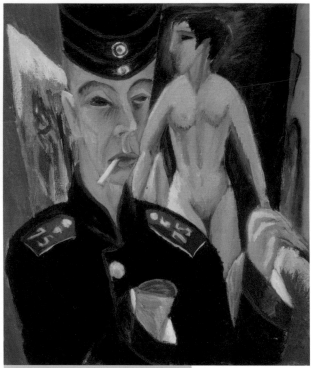

Self-portrait as a Soldier (1915)
by Ernst Ludwig Kirchner
Allen Memorial Art Museum, Oberlin, USA

Born: 6th May 1880
Died: 29th July 1938
Place of Birth: Aschaffenburg, near Dresden, Bavaria, Germany
Family details: He was the eldest son of Maria and Ernst Kirchner. His father was a successful engineer and chemist and both parents came from well off business families in Brandenburg. He had two younger brothers, Walter and Ulrich.
Paintings analysed:
Standing Nude with Hat, 1910
Potsdamer Platz, Berlin, 1914

ERNST LUDWIG KIRCHNER

Childhood

Ernst Kirchner was a sensitive and imaginative child who was apt to have panic attacks. When he was 7 years old, the family moved from Frankfurt to Switzerland and lived near Lucerne for three years. In 1890, his father became a professor in paper research and the family moved back to Chemnitz in Germany. Kirchner went to the local Grammar school but, early on, his parents saw that he was gifted in drawing and set up private lessons for him.

Youth and early career

Kirchner's parents did not want him to follow an artist's career and, in 1901, they made him study for a degree in Architecture at the Saxon Technical College in Dresden. In 1903, he took some time out to go to classes in applied and fine art at the Munich Technical College. Whilst he was there, Kirchner learnt about the new *Art Nouveau* design ideas called *Jugendstil*. He also saw the wonderful prints of the 15th century artist, Albrecht Durer, and learnt how to do the woodcut technique himself. He was inspired by one of his teachers, Hermann Obrist, who thought that art should be experienced as 'intensified, poetic life'.

The forming of the Die Brücke artists group

In 1905, Kirchner finished his degree in Architecture. Whilst on the course he had made good friends with three other men who also wanted to give up architecture and become painters. Their names were Fritz Bleyl, Erich Heckel and Karl Schmidt-Rottluff. Together they founded the group called *Die Brücke* (The Bridge), on 7th June, 1905. They were all impressed by the writings of the

German philosopher, Friedrich Nietzsche, who thought that people should rely more on their instincts than their intellect. In his book called *Thus Spake Zarathustra* (1883–1885), Nietzsche wrote, 'What is great in Man is that he is a bridge and not a goal' and this gave the young men the idea for the name of their new group – The Bridge.

The next year, in 1906, Kirchner wrote down the group's aims which were, 'We want to acquire freedom for our hands and lives, against the well-established older forces. Everyone belongs to us who renders in an immediate and *unfalsified* way everything that compels him to be creative'. The Die Brücke artists wanted their paintings to be expressive and *spontaneous*. They led colourful lives which were shockingly *bohemian*.

The young artists shared a studio in Dresden and lived and worked together. In the early days of the group, the artists were very influenced by the work of the *Post-Impressionists*. Kirchner was deeply impressed by Van Gogh's passionate paintings of nature when he saw them for the first time in 1905. In 1908, a large exhibition of the French *Fauve* painter, Henri Matisse, was organised in Berlin and this also had a big impact on the Die Brücke artists.

In 1906, the Die Brücke group had its first exhibition in the Seifert lamp factory in Dresden. They invited friends and supporters to become what they called 'passive members' of their group. For a small annual donation they received a report of the group's activities and a folder of original prints called the *Brücke-Mappen*. In this way they hoped to draw attention to their work and reach more people.

The group worked closely together. They wanted to overthrow stale, *bourgeois* attitudes and express a new sense of freedom in their work. Their main theme was the nude and each summer they went to the Moritzburg Lakes and there painted themselves and their friends in a natural environment, unspoilt by industrialisation. **Nudes Playing under a Tree**, 1910, is one of Kirchner's paintings from this period.

unfalsified – true, direct and honest.

spontaneous – immediate.

bohemian – a bohemian lifestyle is one which does not keep to the accepted standards or rules in society and is morally free and easy.

bourgeois – a word used to describe the merchant and middle classes and those who keep to conservative and unimaginative social norms in order to keep their power and position in society.

Nudes Playing Under a Tree (1910) by Ernst Ludwig Kirchner
Private Collection

dynamic / dynamism – full of movement, spirited and powerful.

Development of Kirchner's career in Berlin

In 1911, Kirchner left Dresden and went to the capital city of Berlin. His brushwork became more *dynamic* and his shapes bolder and more angular. He started painting scenes from the circus such as **Negro Dance**, 1911, to express life lived at a higher intensity. In the same year, he set up an art school called MUIM with his friend, Max Pechstein, but it closed after a short while.

In 1912, Kirchner met Erna Schilling who was to become his lifelong companion. He also met and painted a portrait of Expressionist writer Alfred Doblin who wrote a famous novel about life in the German metropolis called *Berlin Alexanderplatz*. Kirchner began to get known at the *avant-garde* Der Sturm (The Storm) gallery, and he and the *Die Brücke* group exhibited work with the *Blaue Reiter* group in Munich. They also had a large show in Hamburg and took part in the international Sonderbund Exhibition in Cologne (see page 9).

Red Elisabeth Embankment, Berlin (1912) by Ernst Ludwig Kirchner
Bayerische Staatsgemaldesammlungen, Munich, Germany

At this time Kirchner became more independent from the Die Brücke group and started a new series of work based on views of the city. **Red Elisabeth Embankment, Berlin**, 1912, is one of the most striking paintings of this period. In 1913, Kirchner wrote a Chronicle of the Die Brücke group in which he gave himself all the credit for their ideas. The other members were very upset and the Die Brücke group of young artists came to a bitter end. Many years later in 1926, Kirchner seemed to regret losing the support of his friends and painted a picture of them together called, **An Artists' Group: Otto Mueller, Kirchner, Heckel, Schmidt-Rottluff**, 1926–1927. In it Kirchner is on the left pointing to the Chronicle.

An Artists' Group: Otto Mueller, Kirchner, Heckel, Schmidt-Rottluff (1926–1927) by Ernst Ludwig Kirchner
Wallraf-Richartz Museum, Cologne

By 1913, Kirchner had started on his famous series of street life in Berlin. **The Street**, 1913, shows a change in his style which has energetic brushstrokes and aggressive, pointed shapes. He was becoming well-known in the artistic and intellectual circles of Berlin and began having one-man shows. In 1914, he had an important solo exhibition at the Jena Art Association and took part in the Werkbund Exhibition in Cologne.

The Street (1913) by Ernst Ludwig Kirchner
Brucke Museum, Berlin, Germany

Outbreak of World War I and the effect on Kirchner of the war years

Unluckily, at this high point in Kirchner's career, World War I broke out in August 1914, and he joined the German army. The next year he became very ill and suffered a nervous breakdown. His shocked reaction to the horrors of war can be seen in his **Self-Portrait as a Soldier**, 1915, where he shows his painting hand brutally cut off from his body (see page 28).

His woodcut illustrations of *The Strange Story of Peter Schlehmil, 1814,* by Aldebert von Chamisso, which Kirchner finished in 1915, show Kirchner's tormented state of mind. The story tells of a man who sold his own shadow and placed himself outside human society as a result. Kirchner poured his feelings into this series of prints and **Struggles (The Torments of Love)** and **Schlehmil in the Loneliness of his Room** are powerful examples of Expressionist art. They have become one of the major printmaking achievements of the 20th century.

Kirchner spent most of the war years until 1918 in hospitals getting over nervous illnesses and drug addiction. In 1917, he left Germany and went to get treatment in Switzerland where he lived until the end of his life.

Struggles (The Torments of Love) (1913) by Ernst Ludwig Kirchner
© by Dr. Wolfgang & Ingeborg Henze-Ketterer, Wichtrach/Bern

Development of Kirchner's career in Switzerland

Between 1918 and 1923 he completed a series of striking views of the mountain landscapes in the Swiss Alps. **Stafelalp in the Moonlight**, 1919, is one of the most dramatic images from this period.

Kirchner continued producing lots of paintings and prints and had some of his work made into tapestry designs. In 1921, he had a major exhibition in Berlin and in 1923 in Basel, Switzerland. In 1926, he returned to Germany for the first time since the war. He was asked to do some wall paintings in the new Museum Folkwang in the city of Essen but, after making several sketches, the project collapsed because of the new art policies introduced by the *Nazis* in 1933.

End of Kirchner's career

Up until 1937 Kirchner continued to take part in many international exhibitions in America, Brussels and Italy. However, in Germany in 1937 Hitler and the Nazi party were in power. They hated Kirchner's work and took 639 paintings and prints out of the museums in Germany. They displayed 32 of Kirchner's paintings in an exhibition in Munich labelled *Entartete Kuns* or *Degenerate Art*.

Much of Kirchner's work was destroyed by the Nazis and Kirchner was expelled from the Prussian Academy of Arts. Kirchner fell into deep despair and committed suicide on 10th May, 1938, one year before the start of World War II.

Standing Nude with Hat, 1910, by Ernst Ludwig Kirchner

Stadelsches Kunstinstitut, Frankfurt, Germany

Background

One of the Die Brücke group's aims was that their paintings should be spontaneous and expressive. Their models moved around the studio posing naturally so that the artists could make quick sketches from different viewpoints. This trained Kirchner to look for the simple but essential shapes and forms in the human figure.

In 1908 there was a big exhibition in Berlin of the *Fauve* paintings of Henri Matisse. Although Kirchner denied any influence, it is clear from paintings like **Girl under a Japanese Parasol**, 1909, that he learnt a great deal from Matisse's use of space, colour and line. In **Standing Nude with Hat**, 1910, he created a striking image of a nude set against the *vibrant* colours and bold patterns he had seen in Fauvist paintings.

Kirchner was also excited by art from different cultures. He often visited the Dresden Museum of *Ethnology* and admired the carved and painted wooden beams from the South Pacific island of Palau as well as the African sculpture. The artist's studio was hung with brightly coloured batik and embroidered curtains and full of hand-carved furniture and wooden sculptures. **Standing Nude with Hat**, 1910, was painted during this time of great experimentation.

Ideas

- Ask a friend to move around the room holding different poses for no more than ten minutes at a time. When the model stops make quick sketches using charcoal and try to capture the pose in simple lines.

- If you are studying textiles, design your own fabric based on *traditional* African patterns or carvings from the South Pacific. Make your patterns bold and brightly coloured.

- Kirchner was very interested in African sculptures and carved his own figures from wood. **Standing Female Figure** (1912) is a good example and shows how Kirchner simplified the forms of the human figure in order to create a bold sculpture. Try carving or modelling your own figures out of clay.

- Kirchner was very enthusiastic about the woodcut printing technique. Using this process he often made posters for exhibitions (**Exhibition poster of Die Brücke**, 1910). Design your own poster using strong colour contrasts.

If you do not have any wood, try lino cuts.

34

Standing Nude with Hat, 1910, by Ernst Ludwig Kirchner

Content

The model for this painting was Kirchner's girlfriend, Doris Grosse, whom he called 'Dodo'. She was the most important woman in Kirchner's life from 1908 to 1911. Her pale, white figure stands in front of a brightly coloured curtain which Kirchner had decorated himself. She is wearing a large, wide-brimmed hat and red slippers. Behind her there is a room in which there are paintings of couples together, a bed and tribal objects such as a mask and a large pot.

Kirchner wrote about his girlfriend, 'You gave me the power of speaking about your beauty in the purest image of a woman, compared with which Cranach's Venus is an old crone'. The **Venus** he is talking about was painted by the German artist, Lucas Cranach the Elder in 1532, and a reproduction of this picture hung in Kirchner's studio. Kirchner admired the work of 'old masters', but also wanted to challenge their rules of proportion and 3-dimensional shading.

Another influence was Gauguin's paintings of women in exotic settings on the island of Tahiti, see page 12. In 1910, there was an exhibition of Gauguin's work at the Galerie Arnold in Dresden and Kirchner designed the poster for it.

Form

This large painting shows a lifesize image of Kirchner's girlfriend, Dodo. Her white body stands out against the bright yellows and greens of the curtain behind. Even though Kirchner has drawn Dodo with only a few black lines and no shading, the figure still looks 3-dimensional. The tilt of her head, pose of her arms in front of her body, her necklace and bangle all help to make her appear solid and able to take up space.

At the same time, she also looks like a flat shape and part of the overall patterned surface of the picture. The black shape of her hat is like one of the dark triangles in the curtain behind and her shoes are flat red shapes. Whilst her body looks soft and fragile it is also made up of angular shapes.

When Kirchner was trying to find his own individual style he took in ideas from many different sources. He came across illustrations of figure paintings on Indian temples in an archaeological magazine and made line drawings from them. He wrote about these figures, 'They are all surface and yet absolutely bodies, and thus have completely solved the mystery of painting'. This could easily be a comment made about his drawing of Dodo in this painting.

Process

Kirchner has drawn the figure of Dodo with a few simple lines. In 1920, he called these drawings his *hieroglyphs* because they described natural forms in simple shapes rather than detailed forms. Kirchner thought this way of recording things was more direct and allowed him to express his own feelings and emotions more.

Kirchner mixed petrol with his oil paints so that he could spread them thinly onto large canvases and so that they would dry to a matt finish. He used the paint straight from pots rather than from a palette and painted bold flat areas of vivid colour.

Mood

Kirchner wrote with passion about this picture of his girlfriend, Dodo, who was a designer and maker of hats, saying, 'You, Dodo, with your diligent hands. Still and fine and so palely beautiful. Your fine, free lust for love, with you I experience it to the full, almost at the risk of my destiny'.

This is a striking and exotic image of a woman. In one way, her white body appears delicate and vulnerable beneath the enormous black hat. In another way, she appears strong and forthright, looking directly towards us and surrounded by brightly coloured patterns.

Potsdamer Platz, Berlin, 1914, by Ernst Ludwig Kirchner

Staatliche Museen zu Berlin - Nationalgalerie / Joerg P.Anders / bpk Berlin

Ideas

- Take photos and make drawings of city views. Afterwards, try changing the atmosphere of your drawing by *distorting* the *perspective* and making the shapes in it more pointed and angular.

- Use these drawings as the basis of paintings. Experiment with different colour combinations to alter the mood of your views of the city. Bring people into your work but draw them using sharply angled shapes.

- Try making a drawing of a city street on a slab of clay. Then cut into the clay breaking down the scene into angular shapes across the surface.

Background

In 1911, Kirchner went to live in Berlin (see page 31). There he became friendly with the artist, Max Pechstein (1881–1955), who introduced him to other artists and writers.

Although Kirchner was excited by the *dynamism* of city life, he hated how false, lonely and threatening city life could be. Every summer, he went to the island of Fehmarn and painted lively pictures of a carefree life at one with nature, such as **Figures Walking into the Sea**, 1912.

However, mostly he was in Berlin. The Die Brücke group was falling apart and Kirchner was producing work on his own. He began developing a more aggressive and angular style to express city life. He painted pictures of the city's entertainment like **Girl Circus Rider**, 1912 and vivid city views such as **Red Elisabeth Embankment, Berlin**, 1912 and **Potsdamer Platz**, 1914.

dynamic / dynamism – full of movement, spirited and powerful.

exaggerated – overstated and emphasised.

alienating – alienating experiences create feelings of loneliness and detachment.

distort, distortion – to twist or stretch something into a different shape to deform it.

garish – jarring, harsh and discordant.

Content

This is a large canvas measuring 200cms x 150cms. Two women fill most of the left side of the picture. Their figures are *exaggerated* and extremely tall, stretching from the bottom edge to the top of the painting. They are wearing hats decorated with exotic feathers and are balanced on a round traffic island in one of the main squares of Berlin.

Behind them the acid green streets are haunted by faceless men in dark suits. One man is just about to stride towards the women. He has just stepped off a triangular shaped pavement which juts out into the road.

The buildings are drawn at steep angles and lean towards each other creating narrow, cramped streets which wind away into the background.

It is one of a series of striking Berlin street scenes which are now thought of as his most mature and famous works.

Form

The two women are perched like exotic birds on the round island which is tilted up at a steep angle. Their bodies are made up of hard, geometric shapes and their faces are like masks with blank expressions. They are standing apart from the men behind and one of them is wearing a black veil which makes her look like she is inside a cage.

The men's bodies are stiff and awkward. They look threatening with their dark suits and blank faces. In Kirchner's painting called **Friedrichstrasse, Berlin** (1914), completed just before the beginning of World War I, the men line up behind the women like faceless soldiers or cogs in a horrible machine. Kirchner found city life unnatural and *alienating*. He felt that the experience of crowded city life was brutal and made people lose their identity.

Both the shapes and the colours in this painting make us feel uneasy and tense. The buildings behind the women are squashed together and the space is *distorted*. Pointed shapes jut into the road which is a horrible, acid green. The *garish* red building in the background makes an ugly contrast with the green of the road.

Process

Kirchner has used *garish* and disturbing colour combinations. The bright red of the building clashes with the acid green of the road and the pavements are edged with a vivid blue.

Kirchner slashes the canvas with his brushstrokes and creates jagged edges around the women. He used this technique in other paintings in the city series like **The Street** (1913). See page 32.

Kirchner was very skilful at making woodcut prints in black and white and often produced prints based on his paintings. His rough way of cutting into the wood in parallel lines created a dramatic effect and Kirchner uses the same method to make marks with his paintbrush. These striking, feathered markings can be seen in his expressive portrait of the art dealer Ludwig Schames, completed in 1918.

Mood

This painting has an uneasy and menacing mood. The people in it do not relate to each other. The women are like strutting birds of prey whilst the faceless, dark figures of men prowl around in the background.

Most of the shapes in the painting are pointed and aggressive. Kirchner has constructed a space which seems squashed in on itself and this makes us feel tense and anxious.

Photograph of Wassily Kandinsky

Born: 4th December 1866
Died: 13th December 1944
Place of Birth: Moscow
Family details: Kandinsky's father was a tea merchant in Moscow. His parents divorced when he was five years old. He was brought up by his aunt but both his parents were always devoted to him. He was their only child.
Paintings analysed:
Improvisation 9, 1910
Improvisation 26, (Oars), 1912

WASSILY KANDINSKY

Childhood

Wassily Kandinsky came from a wealthy Russian family. He spent most of the first five years of his life in Moscow and then the family went to live in a town on the coast called Odessa. Sadly, soon after this, his parents divorced.

Wassily was then brought up by his aunt who introduced him to watercolour painting and encouraged his love of fairytales. Both his parents encouraged his musical talent and he could play the cello and piano from an early age.

Youth

In 1886, he started to study Economics and Law at the University of Moscow, which was his favourite city in Russia. He was very successful and was asked to research the peasant laws in country areas of Russia. The folk art and peasant costumes he saw in northern Russia made a lasting impression on him. In 1892, Kandinsky became a lecturer in Law at Moscow University and married his cousin, Anya Chimiakin.

In 1896, he was offered a job as a professor in Law at Tartu University. He seemed set for a successful career but his love of art and music had never left him. He wanted to express all his ideas and experiences in a more creative way and decided to become an artist. At the age of 30, Kandinsky gave everything up and went with his young wife to Munich in Germany to study art.

Early career in Art

In Munich, Kandinsky studied under well-respected German artists such as **Anton Azbe**, and **Franz von Stuck**. He became interested in the new *Jugendstil* or *Art Nouveau* way of designing (see page 7), and, by 1901, he was taking part in exhibitions. He was also getting to know artists who were later to become famous like **Paul Klee** and **Alexis von Jawlensky**.

Kandinsky felt that the Munich Academy's way of teaching art was stifling his creativity and soon branched out on his own. He helped to set up a group of artists called the **Phalanx**. They started their own School of Painting and organised several exhibitions. Kandinsky produced designs for material, jewellery, ceramics and furniture and made woodcut prints in the *Art Nouveau* style.

In 1903, Phalanx showed 16 paintings by the French Impressionist painter **Claude Monet**. Kandinsky was deeply moved by Monet's series of **Haystack**, 1890, paintings and loved his glowing colours. In 1904, Phalanx organised an exhibition of Post-Impressionist painters which included **Paul Signac**, **Vincent Van Gogh** and **Henri de Toulouse-Lautrec**. This was another big influence on his work.

By this time, Kandinsky had split up from his wife, and from 1903 to 1908, he travelled Europe with the painter **Gabrielle Munter**. He showed his paintings and prints in many exhibitions, including the *Salon d'Automne* and *Salon des Indépendants* in Paris. He saw there the work of the Post-Impressionist artists, **Gauguin** and **Cézanne**, as well as new *avant-garde* French artists such as **Henri Matisse** and the *Fauves*, and **Pablo Picasso** and the *Cubists*.

Development of Kandinsky's career

Picture with Archer (1909) by Wassily Kandinsky
Museum of Modern Art (MOMA), New York.
© ADAGP, Paris and DACS, London 2004

Picture with Black Arch (1912) by Wassily Kandinsky
Musee National d'Art Moderne, Centre Georges Pompidou, Paris. © ADAGP, Paris and DACS, London 2004

In 1908, Kandinsky and Munter stopped travelling and bought a house in the small mountain town of Murnau in Bavaria, Germany. They were joined by other artists including Alexei von Jawlensky. Kandinsky explored his ideas about colours and wanted his paintings to be more abstract like music. He produced many beautiful paintings based on the landscape such as **Mountain Landscape with Village**, I, 1908, **Murnau – The Garden**, II, 1910 and **Picture with Archer**, 1909.

In 1910, he met the painter Franz Marc and they became close friends. They both had ideas on the way art should be going and produced a magazine or almanac of their theories on art called *Der Blaue Reiter* (*The Blue Rider*). They called it this as Marc loved horses and Kandinsky thought blue was a heavenly, spiritual colour. Kandinsky designed the cover for the almanac which was a drawing in ink and watercolour of a knight galloping on a horse.

The Blue Rider group organised major exhibitions which showed their own work, as well as a wide range of other artists' work including: Kirchner and the Die Brücke artists; Picasso, Robert Delaunay and the *Cubists*; *Fauve* artists like Maurice de Vlaminck; and many more. The first Blue Rider exhibition took place in 1911 and the second early in 1912.

Kandinsky was becoming very well-known and took part in many exhibitions in Europe, including a solo exhibition at the *avant-garde* Berlin gallery called Der Sturm (The Storm). In 1913, he exhibited in the famous Armoury Show in New York.

Kandinsky was a huge influence on other artists, not only through his paintings but also his writings. In 1911, he wrote *On the Spiritual in Art* and, in 1912, *On the Question of Form*. Kandinsky was moving more and more towards *abstract art* in paintings like **Picture with Black Arch**, 1912.

In 1913, Kandinsky published his latest ideas in *Painting as Pure Art*. He also wrote plays and poems. A photograph taken of Kandinsky at his writing desk shows a very different type of man from the *bohemian* leader of the Berlin *Die Brücke* Expressionist group, **Ernst Kirchner**. Kandinsky was not only a gifted artist and musician but was also a serious thinker who wrote in depth about the theory and *philosophy* of his art (**Photograph of Wassily Kandinsky at his desk in his Munich flat**, 1913, see page 38).

bohemian – a bohemian lifestyle is one which does not keep to the accepted standards or rules in society and is morally free and easy.

philosophy – study of human knowledge and understanding about the underlying principles of the purpose of life.

Kandinsky's career after World War I

When war broke out in 1914, Kandinsky had to leave Germany and return to Russia. His partner, Gabrielle Munter, stayed in Germany and they split up in 1916. In 1917, he married Nina Andreevsky, and had a baby son who sadly died three years later. Kandinsky and Nina stayed together for the rest of their lives.

After the Russian Revolution in 1917, there were lots of exciting things happening in the art world in Russia. Kandinsky worked with new artists' groups such as Tatlin and the *Constructivists*, and Malevich and the *Suprematists*. In 1919, he became the Director of the Museum for Artistic Culture and organised exhibitions of young artists' work, including the First State Exhibition in Moscow. He became a professor at the State Art Workshops and helped to found the Moscow Academy of Arts.

Kandinsky disagreed with the importance given to industrial design in Russia, so in 1921, he returned to Germany where he started teaching at the famous *Bauhaus* Art School in Weimar. There he carried on developing his design ideas. His paintings became more geometrical as in **Composition VIII**, 1923. Kandinsky's work had changed a lot from the paintings of his earlier Expressionist period in Munich and Murnau.

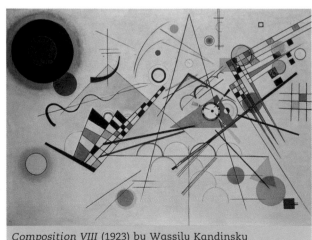

Composition VIII (1923) by Wassily Kandinsky
Peggy Guggenheim Collection, Venice. © ADAGP, Paris and DACS, London 2004

Bauhaus – the Bauhaus was a school of design set up in Germany in 1919 by Walter Gropius. The teachers included Kandinsky and Klee. The Bauhaus style mixed fine art with geometric and simple design. The school was closed down by the Nazis in 1933.

intuition, intuitive – insight and inner understanding.

Yellow-Red-Blue (1925) by Wassily Kandinsky
Musee National d'Art Moderne, Centre Pompidou, Paris, France, © ADAGP, Paris and DACS, London 2004

Around the Circle (1940) by Wassily Kandinsky
Solomon R. Guggenheim Museum, New York, © ADAGP, Paris and DACS, London 2004

In 1924, he formed the Blue Four artists' group with Alexei von Jawlensky, Paul Klee and Lyonel Feininger. In 1925, The *Bauhaus* school moved to Dessau and Kandinsky lived and worked closely with his painter friend, Paul Klee. His work became lighter and more *intuitive* as in **Yellow-Red-Blue**, 1925. He published another important essay called *Point and Line to Plane* in 1926.

The end of Kandinsky's career

In 1933, when the Nazis came to power, the *Bauhaus* was shut down. Kandinsky left Germany and went to live outside Paris where he went on painting until his death in 1944. His later works show softened geometric shapes which have a playful, musical quality (**Around the Circle**, 1940).

Kandinsky's last exhibition before his death was in the Galerie L'Esquisse in Paris. In the last 20 years of his life he was famous around the world and had major exhibitions in most European capital cities as well as New York. His writings and paintings influenced many 20th century artists and were very important to the development of *abstract* art.

Improvisation 9, 1910, by Wassily Kandinsky

Background

In the early 20th century, Kandinsky wanted to find a new purpose and direction for art. He was looking for a more *spiritual* way of showing thoughts and feelings. He thought there was a close link between colour and music and was moved by a performance of *Lohengrin* by the German composer, Wagner, 'I saw all my colours in my mind's eye. Wild lines formed drawings before my very eyes.'.

Kandinsky worked step-by-step towards *abstract compositions* using the basic elements of design – line, shape, and colour. At first he based his work on powerful forms in the landscape as well as his own deeply felt memories and *intuitions* about colour. When he went to live in Murnau, a small town in the mountains of Bavaria, he began a series of landscape paintings which were really a powerful means to express his new ideas on colour and form. One day, he saw one of his own paintings on its side and was struck by its wonderful rhythms and glowing colours. This made him even more sure that a painting did not have to be about real things but that forms and colours could be just as expressive. In 1910, he completed **Improvisation 9**.

Ideas

- Make a painting of a landscape near you. Afterwards, make a series of studies from it, in which the shapes become more simple and *abstract*. You can also make your landscape the setting for a fairytale like Kandinsky did, but be careful not to put in too much of the story. Just add enough detail to make it interesting for the viewer and to create a magical scene.

- Make a collection of rocks and pebbles of different sizes and shapes. Arrange them on a table so some of them are on top of others and they all press up against each other. Draw your arrangement and then outline the shapes in black paint. Paint within these areas with thin patches of paint being careful to see how different colours look when they are put next to each other.

- If you are doing textiles on your course, make up a design for a tapestry from either of these starting points. Use heavy weight threads for the black lines and dots and thinner threads for the patches of colour.

Content

In **Improvisation 9** Kandinsky shows a rider on horseback perched on top of a mountain. A deep valley separates him from another mountain with a castle on top. The sky looks stormy with a black zigzagging line and reddish clouds. The horse's head stretches forward and his front leg scratches at the ground.

Kandinsky was inspired by the folk craft of glass painting which was popular in Murnau. He loved these strong and simply coloured pictures which reminded him of the folk art he had seen in Russia where he was born. Kandinsky had always adored Russian and German fairytales and had already used them to create enchanting scenes like **Couple Riding**, 1906, and **Lancer in Landscape**, 1908.

Kandinsky admired the transparent, clear colours of the glass painting technique and painted his own pictures on glass such as **Glass Painting with Sun**, 1910. He sketched in a magical world of castles and horse-riders with black painted lines and then brushed on patches of colour.

Process

Kandinsky wanted his paintings to be understood in the same way as we listen to a piece of music. To use musical terms, the main *chord* of this *composition* is the dominant purple colour offset by bright yellows and apple greens. A secondary *chord* is made up by areas of blue and its complementary opposite, orange. Areas of deep red and dark green bring all the other colours together into a *harmonious composition*.

Kandinsky arranges patches of thinly spread colour across the whole canvas in such a way that your eye travels around the picture following the rhythms created by each colour. For example, areas of apple green take your eye along the bottom edge of the painting, up to the top of the mountain and across to the castle rooftops.

Within the individual sections of his picture, Kandinsky creates a *rhythmic* feeling by using short, swift brushstrokes to build up overlapping patches of colour. The black dots and zigzag lines make the picture *dynamic* and exciting.

Form

Although we can still make out a scene in this painting, Kandinsky is more interested in the expressive effects he can produce through line and colour. He is not trying to describe an actual landscape or storyline but to create a powerful picture of *rhythmic* forms, *dynamic* lines and dots, and areas of strong colour.

Kandinsky's shapes press in on each other and swell up like waves in a stormy sea. This sense of movement is continued in the zigzagging line in the sky. In earlier paintings like **Picture with Archer**, 1909 (see page 41), Kandinsky's forms are even more *turbulent* and his dark colours create a feeling of conflict and struggle.

Kandinsky outlines the main shapes in black. In this way, he breaks up the large canvas into smaller sections which helps to organise the different areas of colour. These sections do not always relate to things in a real landscape but are independent shapes used by Kandinsky to create a bold design.

Within each large section, Kandinsky brushes on smaller areas of colour which overlap each other and blend together. This creates a lively surface which produces smaller rhythms and movement throughout the picture.

Mood

This is a *vibrant* painting which makes us feel like we are looking into a magical and *spiritual* world of glowing colour.

Like the *Post-Impressionist* artists, Vincent Van Gogh and Georges Seurat, Kandinsky believed that colour and line could act directly on our state of mind. He wanted the people who saw his paintings to achieve a state of *spiritual contemplation*.

Improvisation 26 (Oars), 1912, by Wassily Kandinsky

Stadtische Galerie im Lenbachhaus, Munich, Germany, © ADAGP, Paris and DACS, London 2004

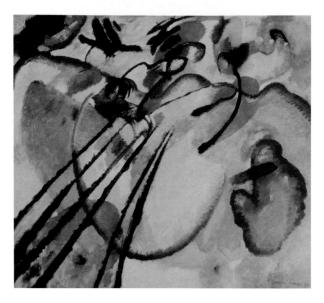

Background

In his work, Kandinsky wanted to explore ideas about *philosophy*, *mysticism*, religion, music and colour. He believed that mankind was on the brink of a new spiritual age. He felt that this could be best expressed in art by using a more *abstract* language of colour and form.

Kandinsky and Marc were convinced that their group, Blue Rider (see page 41), was not just a new movement in painting but was a call for spiritual renewal in all spheres of art and culture. The Blue Rider almanac included lots of illustrations from Chinese paintings to Egyptian art and children's drawings. Paintings of the Blue Rider group were shown alongside Post-Impressionist work. There was also music and writing from modern composers and leading Expressionist artists. Kandinsky said that in each work, the artist had tried his best to express an 'inner wish' or feeling. Kandinsky's paintings moved further away from the depiction of real places and things and more towards expressive *abstraction*. In 1912 he completed **Improvisation 26 (Oars)**.

calligraphy – beautiful and decorative handwriting.

hieroglyphs – a drawn symbol which represents something in a way which is brief and to the point.

motif – dominant idea and subject.

turbulent – stormy and tempestuous.

prophetic – containing a prediction or description of what will happen in the future.

Content

Most of Kandinsky's paintings of this period are not total *abstractions*. He had favourite themes and a personal language of shapes and forms which had developed in previous work.

In the years leading up to the outbreak of World War I, Kandinsky often painted pictures on the themes of flood and catastrophe. **Improvisation 26** has black lines and shapes which suggest people in a boat, rowing with long black oars in a sea of swirling colours. Rowing boats were one of Kandinsky's favourite *motifs* at this time. They were probably symbols of forward movement as well as showing how vulnerable people were in the face of the great forces in nature.

The overall effect of **Improvisation 26** is much calmer than the paintings that came after. In 1913, Kandinsky's series of paintings on floods and disasters were far more violent and unsettling. Kandinsky's colours become darker and more threatening in **Flood Improvisation**, 1913, and **Composition VI**, 1913, in which we can only just make out the shapes of boats and oars being tossed about among swirling, chaotic shapes.

Process

Kandinsky spreads the oil paint thinly onto the canvas. The areas of colour seem to float across the painting, sometimes blending into each other, and sometimes moving away from each other. The main yellow area moves outwards from the large blue area but both colours are linked by the red arc. This creates a sense of movement, space and depth in the painting.

The black lines of the oars are done in thicker paint and are on top of everything else. They come from the centre of the painting and create a feeling of *dynamic* energy.

Kandinsky loved the music of modern composers like Arnold Schonberg. He admired the free *chords* Schonberg played and enjoyed his expressive tonal music. Kandinsky felt he was trying to achieve the same thing in his *abstract* paintings.

Form

The rowers in the centre of the picture are drawn with swift black lines. Kandinsky admired *calligraphy* and included illustrations of Japanese pen and ink drawings in the Blue Rider *almanac*. He developed his own *hieroglyphs* or short forms to suggest things that he often used in his pictures such as the rower, boat, horse rider, knight battling with a lance, or hills in a landscape.

In **Improvisation 26**, Kandinsky has not surrounded the areas of colour with black outlines as they were in his earlier paintings such as **Improvisation 9** (see page 44). Here the black lines and areas of colour are independent of each other and Kandinsky uses them both as powerful means of expression. The colours cover large areas and seem to float across the whole painting.

For Kandinsky, colours were symbolic in themselves. He wrote about the determined and powerful intensity of red and the mystical calmness of blue. The striking black shapes and lines in his work represent energy and sometimes struggle and conflict.

The calm blue areas appear to be withdrawing as the powerful red arc and wavy lines penetrate across the painting. The red shape in the bottom right hand corner looks like another rowing figure but it seems more crouched and threatening. The black lines of the oars streak out from the centre of the painting creating a powerful area of energy and force.

Mood

This painting gives one the feeling of the beginning of a struggle or storm. The energetic lines of the rowers and the looming dark shapes at the top of the painting give a feeling of energy and foreboding.

The red lines penetrate the whole painting. Although the calm blue colours are struggling to come to the surface, they are becoming submerged and moving into the background.

Kandinsky's disaster and flood paintings became more and more *turbulent* and chaotic in 1913 and 1914, and when we look at them now, they seem to foretell the great catastrophe that was going to hit Europe in World War I. His famous stained glass window, **Apocalyptic Horseman** completed in 1914 seems to be truly *prophetic*.

Photograph of Franz Marc
around 1912

Born: 8th February 1880
Died: 4th March 1916
Place of Birth: Munich, Germany
Family details: Marc's father, Wilhelm Marc, was a professor of painting at the Munich Academy. His brother Paul was three years older than him.
Paintings analysed:
Stables (Stallungen), 1913

FRANZ MARC

Childhood and youth

Marc grew up in a very religious family and when he was 17 years old he wanted to become a clergyman. However, before he could start his studies, he was called up for a year's military service. Whilst in the army he learned to ride horses, and he showed his love for these animals in many of his later paintings. By the time he left the army he had decided to become an artist like his father.

Early career

Between 1900 and 1903, Marc studied art and philosophy at the Munich Academy. There he learnt to paint landscapes like **Cottages on the Dachau Marsh**, 1902, in the *traditional* way with lots of detail and *naturalistic* colours such as greens and browns. In 1903, Marc visited Paris and was very struck by the *Impressionist* paintings he saw there. When he returned to Munich, he gave up the academic style of painting and began using brighter, stronger colours.

In 1905, Marc met the French animal painter, Jean Bloe Niestle, who encouraged him to express his love of animals in his work. He began studying animal *anatomy* at Berlin Zoo so that he could use what he learnt in an imaginative way in his paintings. To raise money, he gave drawing lessons on *anatomy* until 1910. His personal life had been going badly during these years and several relationships had failed, but in 1908 he spent the summer with the painter, Maria Franck, whom he later married in 1911.

tradition, traditional – ways of doing things which are often handed down from one generation to another.

naturalistic – realistic method that attempts to show nature as it is.

anatomy – structure of a body including muscles, skeleton, etc.

Development of his career as an artist

In 1907 Marc visited Paris again and loved the work of the *Post-Impressionists*, **Van Gogh**, **Gauguin** and **Cézanne**. In 1909, he helped to put up an exhibition of Van Gogh's work in Munich and paintings like **Cats on a Red Cloth**, 1909–1910, clearly show the influence of Van Gogh's strong colours and expressive brushwork.

Marc showed this painting in his first solo exhibition held at Brakl's art gallery in Munich. The public and critics liked his work and as a result of the exhibition, he met the artist, **August Macke**, who was to become a lifelong friend. He also met the wealthy industrialist and art collector, Bernard Koehler, who agreed to support Marc for a year if he gave him half of the paintings he produced. This enabled Marc to develop his artistic ideas and style without worrying about money.

Marc spent the summer of 1910 painting with Macke, who encouraged him to use colour in a more expressive way, rather than in a *naturalistic* way. (See the bright colours in a **Horse in a Landscape**.) They visited an exhibition at the Thannhauser Gallery in Munich organised by the New Artists' Association which showed work by *Fauve* artists as well as paintings by **Kandinsky** and **Jawlensky**. Marc was very impressed, and soon after he painted the stunning picture called **Horse in a Landscape**, 1910, using large areas of bright, contrasting colour. Not many critics liked the Munich exhibition but Marc wrote an article praising it and saying, 'Everyone with eyes in their head must here recognise the powerful trend of new art'.

naturalistic – realistic method that attempts to show nature as it is.

Horse in a Landscape (1910) by Franz Marc
Museum Folkwang, Essen, Germany

spiritual – the spiritual involves the inner, expressive side of human understanding.

symbolic / symbolist – a sign or object which stands in for, and refers to, a hidden or deeper meaning. The Symbolist movement involved writers as well as artists. Symbolists were against realism in Art and wanted to create pictures which were more imaginative and dream-like.

abstract / abstraction – abstract art calls attention to shape, colour and form rather than making an object or landscape look recognisable.

As a result of this, Marc met Kandinsky and became a member of the New Artists' Association. Macke, Kandinsky and Marc shared ideas on how to create a new *spiritual* kind of art, the link between music and art, and the expressive and *symbolic* use of colour. They wanted to achieve a 'spiritual awakening' in art and, in June 1911, Kandinsky asked Marc to write and publish a magazine or *almanac* with him. They decided to call it the *Der Blaue Reiter* or *The Blue Rider* because according to Kandinsky, 'We both loved blue, Marc horses and I riders'.

In December 1911, Kandinsky and Marc resigned from the New Artists' Association and organised the first Blue Rider exhibition. The year 1912 was very important, starting with the second Blue Rider exhibition in February and the publication of the Blue Rider *almanac* in May. Marc wrote an article for it called *Spiritual Wealth* in which he said how sad he was that people were more interested in technical advances than *spiritual* ideas.

In the autumn of 1912, Marc went to Paris and met the French painter, Robert Delaunay. Marc was very impressed with the clear colours and *cubist* shapes in Delaunay's window paintings like **Simultaneous Windows on the City**, 1912. He also saw the Sonderbund Exhibition in Cologne and admired the exciting movement in Italian *Futurist* paintings. Both these experiences changed Marc's way of working and he began producing more *abstract* pictures which had complicated structures and layers of colour, such as **Stables**, 1913 (see page 54).

Also in 1913, Marc painted **Animal Destinies** in which the shapes of animals were caught inside pointed, threatening forms. Later on in 1915, when he was a soldier in the German army during World War I, he wrote to his wife about this picture saying, 'It is like a premonition of this war, horrible and gripping. I can hardly believe I painted it!'

Just before the war started in 1914, Marc painted a series of four paintings which were more *abstract* than any he had done before. They were called **Cheerful Forms**, **Playing Forms**, **Forms in Combat** and **Broken Forms**. They also seem to foretell the horror and destruction of the coming war, especially the swirling red and dark blue shapes in **Forms in Combat**, 1914.

Before the war broke out Marc planned to publish an illustrated edition of the Bible with other artists like Wassily Kandinsky, Paul Klee and Oskar Kokoschka. Marc was going to illustrate the Book of Genesis and started producing woodcuts on the Creation story called **Birth of the Horse** (see page 53) and **Birth of the Wolves**.

Forms in Combat (1914) by
Franz Marc
Staatsgalerie Moderner Kunst, Munich, Germany

Animal Destinies (1913) by
Franz Marc
Kunstmuseum Basel

This project was cut short by the start of World War I in August, 1914. Both Marc and his painter friend **Auguste Macke** volunteered at once, but in October of that year Macke was killed. Marc had supported the war effort at the start, but personal tragedies and the terrible destruction and horror he saw at the front, soon changed his mind. Sadly, on 4th March, 1916, he too was killed on the battlefield at Verdun in France.

Soon after Marc's death there were several exhibitions of his work including one in the Berlin Der Sturm Gallery. In 1919, The Berlin National Gallery bought Marc's **Tower of Blue Horses**, 1913, and during the 1920s his work was very well thought of.

Unfortunately, after 1933, when the Nazi party came to power they hated his work along with most of the other Expressionist artists. His paintings were shown in the '*Degenerate Art*' exhibition of 1937 and many of his pictures were taken out of galleries and lost or destroyed. Happily, in 1945 after World War II, his work became very popular again and there was an important exhibition of his work in Munich in 1980.

Birth of the Horse (1913) by Franz Marc
Hamburg Kunsthalle, Hamburg, Germany

Stables (Stallungen), 1913, by Franz Marc

Solomon R. Guggenheim Museum, New York

Background

Franz Marc painted animals because for him they represented everything that was pure, true and beautiful in life. In a letter to his wife he wrote, 'On the whole, instinct has never failed to guide me … especially the instinct which led me away from man's awareness of life and towards that of a "pure" animal'.

Marc wanted to show more than just what animals looked like. In the way he painted them he wanted to express his own deeply *spiritual* ideas about the world. He wanted to show us a vision of their existence in *harmony* with nature.

When he was writing for *The Blue Rider* magazine with Kandinsky, he said his aim was to 'reveal the mighty laws which hold sway behind the beautiful exterior'. He tried to express this in powerful paintings like **Tiger**, 1912 (see page 17), where he merged the form of the tiger with the landscape around. The whole picture is filled with *rhythmic* shapes.

In his article, called *The New Painting*, 1912, Marc said he wanted to express what he called 'the inner spiritual side of nature'. With this in mind, his paintings became more and more *abstract*. Although **Stables** still has horses within it, Marc created a *composition* which relied mostly on shape and colour.

Ideas

- Marc painted his dog, Russi, in **Dog Lying in the Snow**, 1910–1911. In it Marc contrasts the yellow of the dog with patches of deep purple in the snow. Marc often used striking contrasts of *complementary colours* in his animal paintings. **Blue-Black Fox**, 1911, is another stunning example of his use of *vibrant* colour. If you have a favourite animal or pet, try painting it in a similar way to Marc so it looks part of its surroundings and is glowing with colour.

- Make up your own grid of triangles and rectangles and then put in the simplified shapes of animals you like. Paint your design using striking colour combinations.

- If you are doing textile design, your painting could be the basis for a colourful tapestry.

harmonious / harmony – being in agreement, peaceful, not contrasting or jarring.

rhythm, rhythmic – a flow of words, music, or colours and shapes in which there are repeated weak and strong elements.

Content

Marc's favourite animals were horses and he painted many pictures of them. One of the most famous was **The Tower of Blue Horses**, 1913 (see page 53) which he painted around the same time as **Stables**. It shows a series of horses one behind or on top of the other, and has a strong sense of movement.

Late in 1912, Marc had been to Paris where he admired Robert Delaunay's brightly coloured 'window' series of paintings like **Window into Town**, 1912. On the way back he saw an exhibition of the new *Futurist* work by Italian painters such as **Umberto Boccioni**. Both experiences had a big influence on his work and he wanted to achieve the same effect of *dynamic* movement in his own paintings.

In **Stables** we see several views of horses at the same time. The swirling circular shapes and overlapping *planes* give a strong sense of movement.

Form

Marc has drawn a structure of triangles and rectangles which cross over each other. They form a complex grid which reminds us of the architecture of stables in the title of the painting.

Within these geometric shapes you can see different views of horses. Some are repeated, like the back views of horses on the right side of the painting and the curves and circular shapes of the horse's neck, back and tail.

Every line is necessary to the structure of the painting within which Marc has arranged his colours. Areas of red and green (*complementary colours*) are balanced across the picture. They are broken up by patches of yellow and blue. Marc wanted to achieve a *harmony* of colours in his paintings so they would express a new kind of *spiritual* art.

Process

Marc brushed the paint on thinly and the coloured areas look like transparent windows through which you can see the colours beneath.

Marc was not happy using colour in an *intuitive* way alone, so he worked out a system which gave colours particular qualities. For Marc all colours had *symbolic* qualities as well as connections with the natural world. Yellow was feminine and stood for feeling as well as the sun; blue was masculine and stood for spirit as well as the sky; red was brutal and stood for matter and the earth.

Mood

This painting has an exciting sense of movement and at the same time a feeling of structure and order.

The overlapping shapes give a strong sense of depth. They also create an intricate surface pattern of vivid colours.

In his article, *The New Painting*, Marc wrote about the importance of art. He said, 'Nature is everywhere, in us and outside us; but there is something which is not quite nature but rather the mastery and interpretation of nature: art'. In this painting Marc has succeeded in making his own glowing vision of nature. He has created a *harmony* of colours and shapes within a *dynamic* structure.

Glossary

abstract / abstraction – abstract art calls attention to shape, colour and form rather than making an object or landscape look recognizable.

alienating – alienating experiences create feelings of loneliness and detachment.

almanac – annual calendar of months and days. Although Kandinsky and Marc's Blue Rider magazine was called an almanac, in the end they only published one book.

anatomy – structure of a body including muscles, skeleton, etc.

Art Nouveau – the term means 'new art' and this movement spread across Europe and America in the 1890's. It was mainly a style of architecture and interior decoration and was based on flat patterns and organic forms.

avant-garde – a military term which was given to the art movement which was the most recent, shocking and innovative.

Bauhaus – the Bauhaus was a school of design set up in Germany in 1919 by Walter Gropius. The teachers included Kandinsky and Klee. The Bauhaus style mixed fine art with geometric and simple design. The school was closed down by the Nazis in 1933.

Blaue Reiter – The term means Blue Rider. Kandinsky and Marc organized two Blaue Reiter exhibitions in 1911 and 1912. They also published the Blaue Reiter almanac in May, 1912.

bohemian – a bohemian lifestyle is one which does not keep to the accepted standards or rules in society and is morally free and easy.

bourgeois – a word used to describe the merchant and middle classes and those who keep to conservative ways and do not want to change.

calligraphy – beautiful and decorative handwriting.

catalogue – a book which lists artworks displayed in an exhibition and also has essays in it describing and explaining the work.

chord – a group of musical notes which are sounded together.

composition – arrangement of the parts of a picture.

complementary colours – colours opposite each other in the colour wheel which create a vibrant effect when placed near to one another. These complementary colours included red/green, yellow/purple and blue/orange.

Constructivism, Constructivist – an artistic movement in Russia where artists like Vladimir Tatlin and Naum Gabo wanted to 'construct' a new kind of art using abstract shapes and forms.

contemplation – deep thought.

Cubism / Cubists – a style of painting developed in 1908 by Georges Braque and Pablo Picasso. They made paintings which showed things from different angles at the same time and broke up their pictures into geometric shapes like cubes and triangles.

Degenerate Art – the Nazis hated the modern trends in art and called it degenerate which means sinful or corrupt.

Der Blaue Reiter – The term means Blue Rider. Kandinsky and Marc organised two Blaue Reiter exhibitions in 1911 and 1912. They also published the Blaue Reiter almanac in May, 1912.

Die Brücke – means the bridge and was the name given to a group of artists in Germany who wasted ' freedom for their hands and lives'.

distort, distortion – to twist or stretch something into a different shape, to deform it.

Divisionism, Divisionist – a style of painting developed by Georges Seurat and Paul Signac in which colours are split up into dots and dashes of primary colour. When you stand back from the painting you mix the colours visually.

dynamic / dynamism – full of movement, spirited and powerful.

Ethnology – the study of different races and cultures.

exaggerated – overstated and emphasized.

Fauvism / Fauves – comes from a French word meaning 'wild beasts'. In 1905, this name was given to a group of artists led by Henri Matisse who painted using a bold and shocking style with very bright colours.

frescoes – wall paintings.

Futurism, Futurist – the Futurists were a group of Italian artists, such as Giacomo Balla and Umberto Boccioni, who were working around 1909. They loved big cities, speed and machinery and tried to show dynamic movement in their paintings.

garish – jarring, harsh and discordant.

harmonious / harmony – being in agreement, peaceful, not contrasting or jarring.

hieroglyphs – a drawn symbol which represents something in a way which is brief and to the point.

hue – colour, tint.

illusion – when it looks as if something is there but it is not.

intuition, intuitive – insight and inner understanding.

Jugendstil – the art nouveau movement in Germany was called Jugendstil after a magazine called 'Jugend' or 'Youth' which was first published in 1896.

motif – dominant idea and subject.

mysticism, mystical – to do with spiritual and hidden meanings of the occult.

naturalistic – realistic method that attempts to show nature as it is.

Nazis – a fascist political party that came to power in Germany in 1933. Their leader was Adolf Hitler.

New Objectivity – an art movement in Germany which reacted against Expressionism. The main painters were George Grosz, Otto Dix and Max Beckmann. They wanted art to be more realistic and political.

Odalisques – the name given to female slaves from Turkish harems. In Matisse's work the term refers to a series of paintings of reclining women in exotic surroundings.

one-point perspective – a system of perspective in which all the horizontal lines in a picture meet at one point. This point is at the eye level of the viewer and is called the vanishing point.

patrons – people who support artists by promoting and buying their work.

perspective – a way of constructing a picture from a particular viewpoint as though you were looking through a window into it.

philosophy – study of human knowledge and understanding about the underlying principles of the purpose of life.

planes – surfaces, sides or facets.

porcelain – delicate kind of clay from which statues or fine china can be made.

Post-Impressionist – a term given to the artists who came after the Impressionists such as Gauguin, Van Gogh, Seurat and Cézanne.

prophetic – containing a prediction or description of what will happen in the future.

psychology – a study of human behaviour and states of mind.

rhythm, rhythmic – a flow of words, music, or colours and shapes in which there are repeated weak and strong elements.

Salon d'Automne – an exhibition held in Paris in the autumn of each year.

Salon des Indépendants – exhibitions started in 1884 by Seurat and Signac in opposition to the official Salon.

Secessions – groups of artists in Germany and Austria who broke away from the established academies in the 1890's and set up their own styles.

spiritual – the spiritual involves the inner, expressive side of human understanding.

spontaneous – immediate.

Suprematism, Suprematist – a movement of geometric, abstract art started in Russia by Malevich in 1913.

Symbolic / Symbolist – a sign or object which stands in for, and refers to, a hidden or deeper meaning. The Symbolist movement involved writers as well as artists. Symbolists were against realism in Art and wanted to create pictures which were more imaginative and dream-like.

tradition, traditional – ways of doing things which are often handed down from one generation to another.

turbulent – stormy and tempestuous.

unfalsified – true, direct and honest.

unnaturalistic – unrealistic method that does not attempt to show nature as it is.

vibrant – vivid, thrilling

Timeline

1863   Edvard Munch born

1866   Wassily Kandinsky born

1867   Emil Nolde born

1869   Henri Matisse born

1879   Paul Klee born

1880   Ernst Ludwig Kirchner born

1881   Max Pechstein born

1884   Max Beckmann born

1886   Oskar Kokoschka born

1887   August Macke born

1890   Egon Schiele born

1892   Exhibition of Munch's paintings in Berlin, closed down after one week

1905   First showing of Fauvist works at the Salon d'Automne

1905   Die Brücke (The Bridge) group formed by Kirchner and friends

1911   Kandinsky and Marc form the 'Blaue Reiter' (Blue Rider) and organise their first exhibition

1912   International Sonderbund Exhibition in Cologne, Germany

1912   'Blaue Reiter' almanac published in May and 2nd 'Blaue Reiter' exhibition

1913   Kirchner writes a chronicle of 'Die Brücke' and the group splits up

1914   World War I begins

1914   August Macke killed in the War

1916   Franz Marc killed in the War

1917   Russian Revolution begins

1918   World War I ends

1919   Bauhaus School of Art and Design opens

1933   The Bauhaus is closed by the Nazis

1937   The 'Degenerate Art' exhibition

1939   World War II begins

1944   Kandinsky dies

1944   Edvard Munch dies

1945   World War II ends

1954   Matisse dies

1956   Emil Nolde dies

Resource List

Books for further reading

Expressionism – A Revolution in German Art by Dietmar Elger, Taschen, 1998

The Expressionist by Wolf-Dieter Dube, Thames Hudson, 1972(republished 1996)

Fauvism by Sarah Whitfield, Thames Hudson, 1991

German Painting by Ulrich Finke, Thames Hudson, 1974

Masters of Colour – Catalogue, Royal Academy of Arts, London, 2002

Movements in Modern Art: Expressionism, by Shulamith Behr, Tate Gallery Publishing, 1999

Kandinsky by Francois le Target, Poligrafa, Barcelona, 1986

Wassily Kandinsky – A Revolutionin Painting, by Hajo Dutching, Taschen, 1993

Kirchner – Expressionism and the City, Royal Academy of Arts exhibition catalogue, 2003

Ernst Ludwig Kirchner – On the Edge of the Abyss of Time by Norbert Wolf, Taschen, 2003

Oskar Kokoschka – Exhibition Catalogue, Tate Gallery, London, 1986

Matisse by Volkmar Essers, Taschen, 1987

Franz Marc by Susanna Partsch, Taschen, 2001

Edvard Munch: The Man and the Artist, by Ragna Stang, Gordon Fraser Gallery, London, 1979

Egon Schiele and His Contemporaries, from the Leopold Collecction, Vienna, Prestel, 1989

Useful Websites

Solomon R. Guggenheim Museum, New York
www.gugenheim.org/new_york_index.html

Lenbachhaus Museum, Munich, Germany
www.lenbachhaus,de/

Leopold Museum, Vienna
www.riga.gov.au

Museum of Modern Art, New York
www.moma.org

Tate, London
www.tate.org.uk

www.artchive.com

www.artnet.com

Photographic Credits

Images on these pages appear by kind permission of the following: